FOCUS GOLF

WITH THE MILESTONE MAN

THE **MENTAL** APPROACH

RON STRECK

Focus Golf with the Milestone Man: The Mental Approach
© 2017 by Ron Streck

Published by Insight Publishing Group
contact@freshword.com
www.freshword.com
918-493-1718

Scripture quotation is taken from the Holy Bible, New Living Translation, copyright ©1996, 2004, 2007 by Tyndale House Foundation. Used by permission of Tyndale House Publishers, Inc., Carol Stream, Illinois 60188. All rights reserved. Author emphasis "you" added.

Golfer illustration by Andrew Dale, Hamsham Productions.

ISBN: 978-1-943361-20-5
E-Book ISBN: 978-1-943361-21-2

Library of Congress Control Number: 2016954763

Printed in the United States of America.

ENDORSEMENTS

"For as long as I've known Ron, I've always been envious of his tenacity and ability to score. Ron's book, *Focus Golf with the Milestone Man,* helps to explain the most important aspects of golf's most valuable intangible...attitude! Simple, easy to understand, and applicable to every golfer who loves this game."

—Peter Jacobsen
PGA Tour Player
NBC Golf

"The first time I met Ron he told me he was going to play the PGA Tour. He had confidence like no one I had ever seen. Not only did he play the PGA Tour but he won on every Tour he played on. The PGA Tour three times, Nike Tour, Champions Tour, and European Tour. His book, *Focus Golf with the Milestone Man,* will help any golfer gain the insight on how to get the most out of their ability. Great book!"

—Hank Haney
Famed Golf Instructor
Ron's College Roommate

"Wonderful insights and lessons from a gritty competitor and great champion. If you love golf, you have to read this."

—Denis Watson
PGA Tour Player

"For all of us non-engineers who don't think in terms of planes and angles, Ron's book is perfect, mixing common sense, humor, and some great wisdom into the mindset and attitude necessary to win on the PGA Tour or in your Sunday foursome."

—Ken MacLeod
Publisher, *Golf Oklahoma* magazine

"What a great book—how important and simple a positive mind-set is to helping our golf game. We all can benefit and become better players if we would just think better and focus on our task at hand."

—Rick Reed
Head Golf Professional
Oaks Country Club, OK

"In an era where the technical side of sports is often over coached, Ron Streck gives golfers and all athletes real, practical insight on the mental side. This book is full of incredible tips and strategies that help develop the athlete's mind. I want every athlete I coach to read this book."

—Chad Wilkerson
Head Basketball and Golf Coach
Lincoln Christian School, OK

"Ron's golf concepts not only work for golf but also for leadership and strategic planning. I use his concepts regarding the importance of focusing to help teach strategic planning to leaders of organizations. I have known Ron for over twenty years and I am still learning from him."

> —Rick Todd
> Senior Vice President
> Herschend Family Entertainment

"Like most ministers, I manage the pulpit better than my putter. In fact, the only reason I want to shoot my age is that I hope to live to be 120. But I know great advice when I see it, and that's what my good friend, Ron Streck, has given us in these pages. *Focus Golf with the Milestone Man* is a sweet, compact read from a guy whose heart, like his typical sand shot, is pure and on target. You're gonna love it!"

> —Rev. James Gilbert
> Author of *Storm Chaser:*
> *The Terry Law Story*
> President,
> James Gilbert Ministries, FL

"*Focus Golf with the Milestone Man* is a practical approach that helps one stay in the present, keep the mind quiet, and focus on executing one shot at a time. I have used the principles and lowered my score. Great book. Easy to read."

—Lawrence Field
Club Champion
Southern Hills Country Club, OK

"As an amateur golfer and a longtime friend of Ron, he has brought to my attention with this book to focus for a few moments on every shot I hit. Simple and effective."

—Tom Hilborne
Amateur Golfer

DEDICATION

To MY PARENTS…

Thank you for giving me life and passing on to me your love and passion for the game of GOLF. I am forever grateful for the opportunities you gave me. I love you.

To JULIANE…MY LITTLE PRINCESS

How is it possible that you are twenty-six—my precious little girl that captured my heart? I can still see you running through this house, playing with your brothers. I remember hearing songs about kids growing up and watching them leave thinking, "Lord, please don't let her go far…." The comfort I had then was that the years seemed to stretch far ahead. A hundred years to live. Now you are a grown woman, a wife and mother. Thank you for giving me my first grandson! Logan will be on the golf course with Pops by next summer.

I am so proud of you and all that you have accomplished and become, and for what you stand for. And when I see you with your brothers, I am forever grateful for your relationships. Are there any other brothers and sister that are better friends? All the prayers we prayed for you and your brothers, God has answered. You'll always be my princess, Juliane. Thank you for being my daughter. I love you.

To JUSTIN…MY SONG MAKER

When you were young, I could not imagine you as you are today. Our little fence kicker, always questioning with boldness. God has shaped you into the leader He wants you to be. Your passion and drive for perfection is something to behold. Thank you for the hours and hours of music, although it sometimes sounded like noise. And even for the countless conversations that were over my head about the engineering science production of sound.

I am proud of you, Justin. For the man you have become and I am proud of your talents and your determination to pursue your passion and become an accomplished producer, composer, engineer, and musician. But even more, I admire your heart and compassion for people, your endless quest for knowledge, and how confident you are with your tenacious boldness. Don't ever loose that. You have such a special place in this family, middle child like me. I love you.

To REAGAN…MY SUPER BOY

When I look back on this short season of raising children, a picture of you will always fill my mind. I am so much more mindful now of how quickly the time passes. I absolutely love playing golf with you and against you! You are finally making me bring some game, son. I have always hoped there would be a day when I actually would be trying to beat you, my little boy. But you are not so little anymore at six feet tall! You have only beaten me on one hole so far, and tied me on another. But you can out drive me over and over when I do not try to best you. Keep it up, son. You're almost there, bubba! "For you can do everything through Christ, who gives you strength" (Philippians 4:13).

Exciting things are just around the corner for you. Remember always who you are and whose you are. You have an unlimited future ahead. I'll always be there, in the stands or behind the ropes for you, cheering you and supporting you. I love you.

To JODY…MY LOVE

I thank GOD for you every day. I am amazed at how you blend love and tenderness with a steadfast conviction for truth and justice, oftentimes while facing tremendous adversity. You are like a lion, a tiger, no, wait…I know…a momma bear! "Oh my!" This life ride with you has been an adventure, babe, and the best is still coming. Thank you for always standing by my side, in front of me, behind me, pushing me, blocking me, gently turning me, and always, always being there, loving me. You are my sunshine. My favorite times are with you by my side. I love you.

SPECIAL THANKS… to my cousin, Clay Winfield, for being more like my brother than a cousin.

To GOD ALMIGHTY…Who has blessed me with all these things in this life.

PGA Pro Ron Streck gives Jody Wiland a tip on her golf swing during the Little Light House's Links for Little Ones held recently at Oaks Country Club.
WORLD STAFF PHOTO
BY TOM GILBERT

Little Light House Charity Pro-Am, Oaks Country Club. When Ron met future wife, Jody. Tulsa, OK. 1994. (Photo by *Tulsa World*)

CONTENTS

Sand Saves Leader. Champions Tour, 2005. (Photo by Gregory Shamus/Getty Images)

Foreword

FINALLY, a practical, readable book on a subject most golfers pay little attention to...the mental side! There are too many books on this topic written by psychologists with higher handicaps than yours!

Ron Streck gives us insight from his experience "in the ring." His advice is "battle tested" and is geared to help everyone from the weekend golfer to the aspiring Tour player.

The concepts Ron shares come from a lifetime of competitive golf. He's been a winner at every level, and so is his book!

> —Mike Reid
> PGA Tour Player
> Winner of two Champions
> Tour majors

Mike Reid golf card. 1982.

Ron Streck and
Mike Reid. 1976.

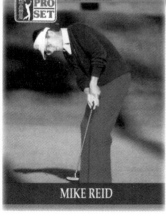

Mike Reid golf card. 1990.

Purpose

Having watched enough high school golf the past couple of years, I saw the critical need for a book to help these young men and women, who love the game, but lack the direction and focus to be great. This is something that affects amateurs too. You do not learn how to hit the golf ball in one lesson. You do not learn to *focus* in one round of golf. It takes practice and repetition.

PGA Tour players positively visualize the shot before they hit it: an image of exactly how they want the ball's trajectory to be, where the ball will land, and a reflection of a previous, successful shot. You hear players talk about coming back from behind in interviews. Having done this gives them the confidence they can do it again. The mind is a powerful force, in golf and in life. And it can be the difference between good and great.

San Antonio Texas Open. A congratulatory hug. Ron Streck with his
mother. 1978.

Introduction

The secret of playing better golf isn't a new driver or a new putter. It's not about a new swing or getting another lesson from your pro. Don't get me wrong, all those things are important, but not nearly as critical to your success on the golf course as your mental frame of mind.

I want to help you narrow the thought process of literally every shot you take on the course from tee to green. I want to help you focus your mind down to one particular positive idea or phrase that will help you silence all those other voices swirling around in your head.

Indeed, you need the physical skills like swing and stance to be correct. But remember, you can have the purest swing of the club, but if your mental game isn't what it should be, you're not going to be as successful as you want to be. A typical swing merely takes a little over a second. If you're an average, amateur golfer, the time spent swinging a club in an entire round is only going to be about two minutes. So in a round of golf that takes about four hours, that's a lot of time for your mind to be free to think whatever it wants to.

3M Championship. Blaine, MN. 2008. (Photo by Kevin C. Cox)

1

It's In Your Head and Heart

The Mental Edge

Let's say you've got two golfers with the same talents and experiences approaching the first tee. Their equipment is similar; they're even wearing the same outfit. Everything about these golfers is the same. Everything, that is, except for one critical ingredient…the mental advantage. One golfer is very confident about his game and approaches the first tee knowing he's going to win this match. The other approaches the tee hoping he doesn't embarrass himself by topping the ball, barely driving it to the ladies' tee box. That image dominates his thoughts as he tees up his ball.

How big of a difference do you think that mental edge will make in the overall round?

It's huge! The guy with the mental advantage is going to beat the other guy 99 times out of 100. I'm the perfect example of that principle at work. I don't have a "classic" golf swing, and I've never led the Tour in putting or greens in regulation. But if we paired up to play a round together, I'm going to defeat you more times than you beat me. Why? It's not necessarily because my game is that much better than yours. But I can almost guarantee, my mental edge is stronger than yours. I don't care if it's golf or Ping-Pong or darts, I am going to win!

The trouble is that the average golfer today is consumed with the physical aspects of his golf game. He seems obsessed with his technique. He's read the latest blog entry by his favorite teaching pro; he's watched the most recent video and consumed the "Tips" section of the latest edition of *Golf Digest*. He approaches the first tee with his head full of different strategies for his grip, stance, swing plane, and club selection. Who knows, he might even be experimenting with a different length of spikes in his shoes. He's grasping at anything that might improve his game and give him an edge over his competitors.

But he's missing the point entirely. When your mind is too clogged up with the physical effort of moving the golf ball around the course, you can't focus on what you need to be doing. Conversely, when you're mentally focused on just one thought or phrase, you can clear your mind, and that's what allows you to relax. That's the whole idea with Focus Golf…to get you to relax on the golf course.

During the 1981 Michelob Houston Open, in the second round, I hit a shot that went through a bunker and came to rest just outside the bunker's edge. This was a difficult lie. My only stance was a left-handed swing. Of course, the problem is that I'm right handed!

I had about sixty feet to the hole, but I had to carry the shot up and over part of the bunker. I turned a wedge upside down to hit the shot. I pulled the shot off! Four feet from the hole, and made par.

I birdied the next three holes and went on to shoot 68 and then a 62 in the final round. I won the tournament by three shots. I attribute that victory to the mental lift I got from that crazy upside-down, left-handed wedge shot. The positivity of that shot carried me to victory. You can't convince me that the mental approach isn't critical in golf.

When we can mentally prepare for a situation, we're much more able to deal successfully with that situation when it happens. Of course, that goes for life as well as for golf. If you prepare your mind positively, your results, more often than not, will be positive. That's why Tour players have been excellent over the years at developing short memories for bad shots, bad holes, and bad rounds. They've become quite skilled at keeping things positive.

Show me two or three golfers at the 19th hole and I can almost guarantee the subject of who's going to be the next Arnie, Jack, or Tiger will come up. I know all three of these great players and I've spent enough time with them to recognize they have the strongest mental games of anyone who has ever picked up a club. The weekend golfer can take away a valuable lesson here. What sets these guys apart from their rivals? It's their ability to focus. I'm sure you've heard the phrase, "Success breeds success." Well, it's also true that positive focus produces positive results.

A Passion for the Game

We know that the ability to focus is what separates the great golfers from the merely good golfers. But there's something else, something much harder to quantify that sets them apart. That "something" is PASSION. By definition, passion is "a strong feeling of enthusiasm or excitement for something or about doing something." When we have a passion for something, it becomes very easy to accomplish it because we're willing to do whatever it takes to improve.

We eat, breathe, and go to sleep every night developing passion. I've been fortunate enough in the course of my career to spend a lot of time with many of the greats of the game. I've been blessed to talk at length with guys like Sam Snead, Byron Nelson, Ben Hogan, Arnold Palmer, and Jack Nicklaus. They all told me that back in the early days of professional golf there was hardly any money at all. Lots of guys had to have a regular job just to help supplement their income. If you wanted to succeed at the game, you needed more than just the winning purse to motivate you to win. You had to have a deep and abiding love for the game to put in the necessary work on the practice range.

In his lifetime, Arnold Palmer has made 100 times the amount of money from marketing, advertising, and designing golf courses than what he ever actually earned playing the game. But it was the competition that fired his passion for golf.

To reach the upper echelons of the game, you have to be willing to put in the hours and hours of work. The time that the greats of the game put into developing their skills is hard for the ordinary golfer to even comprehend. Arnold Palmer used to hit balls until his hands bled. Ben Hogan told me he would practice with just one club all day long. But these players would never call these hours spent practicing, "work." It was their passion for the game that drove them to greatness.

The Michelob Houston Open. Defending Champion
Ron Streck playing in the Pro-Am with former President
Gerald Ford, Bryant Gumble, and Bob Hope. 1982.

2

Competing Against Yourself

The Traffic Jam of Negativity

The mistake I see time and time again with amateur golfers is the pressure they put on themselves by overthinking, especially on the very first hole. Think about it. You're out for a round with your buddies or with someone you want to impress, and the first tee is right there by the clubhouse. Even if it's just a simple Saturday round with no gallery, there are still folks standing around the first tee waiting for their turn to hit. It's only human nature to want to do well, to show everyone just how good at this game you are.

You tee it up and take a moment to stand behind the ball and take in the beautiful scene. You visualize the ball leaving the tee and splitting the fairway on an impressive trajectory, just like the Shot Tracker on television. You bend the shot correctly around the dogleg, and it lands softly, rolling and coming to rest in the perfect spot for your approach to the green. Before the ball even stops moving, you bend over to grab your tee, confident that the shot is the envy of the rest of your foursome, as well as the groups on deck. You place the driver back in your bag, feeling the eyes of everyone on you. Yeah, you hit that shot…just like you knew you could.

But there's a problem. You never get to finish that thought. The vision of that perfect shot is quickly crowded out of your mind. When you look down at the ball, your brain is immediately flooded with negative and even random thoughts. "Don't hit this shot into the trees on the right like you usually do." "Don't overcompensate and pull hook it into the foursome walking up 18." "Wow, the wind sure is blowing hard; I'm going to have to really grip it and rip it." "What is that bee doing on my ball?" "Don't swing too fast." "Don't embarrass yourself!" "Keep your weight balanced." "Is my ball teed up too high?"

Sound familiar? All these thoughts form a gnarly traffic jam in your mind, and now that vision of the perfect tee shot is long gone. As you stand over the ball, you're having trouble pulling back now because you have no idea where this ball is going to go.

The negative thoughts have created tension that causes you to grip the club like you're trying to strangle it. The pressure travels up through your arms to your shoulders and into your neck and back. With all this going on, you stand little chance of hitting the shot you want to hit…the one you visualized when you first came up on the tee.

Of course the real shame of it is when you do eventually hit that ball into the trees, or pull hook into the 18th fairway, or some other equally embarrassing shot, it will immediately be added to the highlight reel in your mind with all your other bad shots—all cued up and ready to play the very next time you stand over your shot.

Putting the Past in the Past

With me, it's different. Golf is my business on the course, though it may be a beautiful place to spend an afternoon, it is simply my office, it's where I work. When I tee it up, I'm not just playing a game. I don't want to just shoot a good score. When I turned pro, playing just for fun was no longer an option. Now I have to shoot a score that pays the bills.

I remember shooting a 66 in the first round of a Tour event in San Diego, even though I'd made an 8 on a par 4 early in the round. When I finished, I was doing a media interview because at the time I was the early leader in the clubhouse. The media had gone over my round and noticed the quad I'd made on the third hole. Instead of talking about all the good shots I'd hit that day, in typical media fashion, they zeroed in on that disastrous third hole. They asked me, "What happened on 3? Why the quad?"

"Well," I said, "I made a five-foot putt for 8." Of course, the line got a few laughs, and they finally moved on and talked about the other things I was able to do that round to shoot a 66. They finally got around to asking me about the eight birdies and the eagle that followed.

My point of that story is that I had already forgotten about the 8 and was looking forward to playing that par 4 the next day (which I did and made par by the way). The last thing I wanted to do was replay the incident. During that first round, I was able to put the quad behind me and shift my focus forward. I made the 8 on the third hole, so there was a lot of golf left to play; I put that out of my head. I didn't think about what the 8 was going to do to my overall score. I was just playing golf, one shot at a time. It never crossed my mind that I wasn't going to be able to shoot a good score that day.

That's why you see Tour players almost always appear calm and collected even with all the pressure on them to perform. You see this, in particular, among the top players. They've had to learn to handle the pressure that comes with the game of professional golf. Handling pressure well is easy to talk about, but it's tough to master this level of concentration without lots of experience. That's why there are so few great golfers in the world at any one time. This game ain't easy!

Some may call it "mental toughness" but I call it focus. Focus is the ability to condense the mountain of thoughts and distractions that invade your mind before each shot into a single positive notion that will help you succeed.

Over the years, I've developed four keys to playing Focus Golf. These keys help narrow the focus from the multitude of thoughts that cloud your mind down to that one, laser-focused, positive thought or word.

My desire is for you to learn the following keys that will help you quickly absorb how to develop a strong mental edge. It's my hope that you'll learn to cast your focus forward and not backward; that you'll learn not to dwell on the bad shots, bad breaks, missed putts, gusty wind, and playing partners needling you.

So, how do you learn to focus?

16th Hole, Royal Golf Dar Es Salam course. Hassan II
Trophy, European Tour, final round. 1983.

Hassan II Trophy, Moroccan Open, European Tour. 1983.

3

Concentrated Effort

KEY #1: Thinking Forward

Have you ever noticed that golfers love to talk about golf? They'll talk about whether Tiger could have beaten Sam in his prime. They'll argue for hours about which course is tougher, Augusta National or Oakmont. And inevitably, they'll talk about the most difficult shots in golf. Is it the high fade, the low cut shot, into the wind par 3, or over water?

You know what I think? I believe the toughest shot in golf is the shot that comes right after a bad shot. It's the most important shot to get right. I've played with a lot of amateurs in my day and the one mistake I see time and time again is that they let the memory of a bad shot bleed over into the next shot and lead to several more bad shots in a row.

And it's not just a problem with amateurs. I've seen pros lose tournaments because they miss a short putt on one hole, causing them to tense up or make a poor decision on the next tee, which causes another bad shot, and now they're on a slippery slope. They look up at the scoreboard and imagine the hoard of golfers breathing down their neck. Then they try to make eagle instead of birdie, and they try to get back all their lost strokes in one hole. Of course, the result is their game goes down the drain. And it's not because they strained their wrist or because they tweaked their back. No, it's mental failure pure and simple. They forgot to THINK FORWARD.

It's natural to stand over your ball and suddenly remember the last time you tried to hit that shot or used that club or played that hole. If the last time you hit your driver you hit it so far into the junk you never found it, it's only natural to be thinking about that shot the next time you pull your driver out of the bag. But that's thinking backward, not forward.

Thinking about the bad shots you've hit that round or about the bogey you made on the last hole are in the past. There's nothing you can do about them now. The only way to redeem those mistakes is to focus on the next shot...thinking forward.

Take the "Amnesia Pill"

Let's say you just finished playing a round where you putted poorly. The worst thing you can do is talk with all your buddies about your failures on the green that day. All that talk only serves to cement those negative images in your mind. Positive, forward-thinking takes a lot of practice. You'll sometimes be midsentence into your story about lipping out that five-footer when you catch yourself. Don't rehash the negative stuff. Believe me; I know from personal experience this is a difficult habit to break, but it's necessary.

I think a lot of golfers would improve their scores dramatically if there were an "amnesia pill" sold in the pro shop. Just pay your green fee, grab the cart key, and take the "amnesia pill." Immediately, you'd forget about every shot the moment you hit it. For once, you'd be playing Focus Golf, only thinking about the shot that is in front of you right now. But alas, there is no "amnesia pill." So what you can't get with a pill is a skill you have to develop.

Of course, it's not just your bad shots that cause you to think backward instead of forward. Have you ever been on a great round, shooting better than you've played in a long time only to crater in the final three or four holes? What was it that caused you to nosedive? I can almost guarantee that the finishing holes weren't that much tougher. No, what happened was instead of thinking about your shot, you began to think about your score, saying to yourself, "Hey, if I keep this up, I can break 80, or I might even shoot my best score ever!" When you're thinking about your score, you're not thinking about the next shot. You're much more inclined to tense up, and that tension is going to cause problems.

When those thoughts flood your mind, you have to force yourself not to think about what you're shooting. You have to discipline yourself just to play the shot in front of you; the one presented to you now.

When I think back on the best rounds of my career, they all have one thing in common. Not the clubs or the playing partners or even the weather. Whenever I played my best rounds, I had no idea where I stood to par because I wasn't paying attention to my score. I had no idea what my score was. I was only trying to get the ball from the tee to the green so that I could make a putt. Honestly, that's all that was in my head. When my focus was good, so was my score.

The Multiplication Effect

There's no doubting the multiplication effect of a mistake. When you're unable to put a bad shot behind you and think forward, it will not only affect your next shot, it'll affect the decision-making process that takes place before your next shot. In that way, one bad shot leads to another and another. And often it's not an "addition mistake" meaning adding one mistake to another. These things tend to multiply, stacked on top of each other. It's bad enough when it happens in a weekend round with friends, but it's much worse when every bad shot takes you further down the leader board…and further back in the tournament!

When you're able to focus your thoughts and think forward it will not only protect your mind from all those thoughts of past bad shots, it will also protect you from all the other distractions that can take you off your game, even distractions that attack you from outside the ropes.

A lot of the pros have a lot of things going on in their personal lives. The game of golf is just one slice of their overall pie. Many of them have businesses of their own. They've got their endorsements they have to keep happy, and their personal brand they're trying to build, which includes foundation work, hospital visits, personal appearances, and a whole raft of other commitments. Even their families can be a distraction in their own way. It can be a welcome distraction, but a distraction nonetheless. It's fairly typical to assume that the tournaments following the birth of a child for a golfer aren't going to be very good. Or if the golfer is going through marriage or business problems or even if he's working with a new caddie, all of these can cause distractions that keep a golfer from thinking forward.

So, is there a mental side to golf? I think we can all agree that there is. Your mental approach begins with learning to THINK FORWARD and that starts before you get to the first tee. Even as you're on the practice tee or putting green getting ready, the things you're filling your mind with are more important than you can imagine.

It might be a cliché, but you have to learn to be positive. Your attitude and frame of mind have to be, "This is going to be a good day, and I can't wait to get out there!" This can be especially difficult when you know the course is tough or when the weather is bad. When the wind is howling, it's easy to think, "Oh boy. This is going to be a long, stressful day." You have to take on the challenge as just that. A challenge to succeed.

Approaching the first tee with that kind of negative mindset is not the way to set yourself up for success. You must stay positive. Remember, when the weather is bad, everyone has to deal with it, not just you. In fact, during my career, inclement weather was often the great equalizer and gave a guy like me a better chance to do well against the field. It's important to stay positive no matter what.

Remember, when you're thinking forward you're focused on the shot in front of you and only the shot in front of you. You're not thinking about the previous shots or the putt that lipped out on the last hole. Mentally you turn around and face forward. All that other stuff is in the past and since you've taken your "amnesia pill," it no longer exists. All that's left to do is to make the shot in front of you right now.

Champions Tour, Commerce Bank Championship, Eisenhower Park. Ron Streck with prize check. East Meadow, New York. 2005. (Photo by Michael Cohen/Getty Images)

4

Do It Right

KEY #2: Practice, Practice, Practice

One of the very first questions I ask amateurs who are struggling with their game is, "How much do you practice?" Inevitably they'll respond, "Practice? I hit a few balls before a round begins and maybe putt for a few minutes to get the feel of the green." I've always thought it's interesting that they don't see the connection. In my mind, it's obvious. If that's all the practice time they're putting in, it's no wonder they aren't playing the kind of golf they've always wanted to.

When people watch the pros play, there's a reason they always seem to say, "They sure make it look easy." The reason it looks so easy is due to the sheer amount of practice time they've logged over the years, hours and hours of hitting balls in all kinds of conditions. It's this commitment to practice that solidifies a repetitive swing and gives pros the confidence they can repeat that exact swing in competition, and under pressure, when it counts the most.

If you were a surgeon and only performed surgery once every two weeks, you wouldn't be nearly as skilled as the doctor who performed several surgeries every day. Which surgeon would you trust with your life? That's what I thought. We've all heard it before, and it's true, practice makes perfect. Or if not perfect, at least practice makes you better.

It's amazing, in any other area of life or sports, you accept the fact that if you want to get better, you're going to have to practice. If you want to be a better accountant, you're going to have to do a lot of accounting. If you want to be a better writer, you're going to have to write…a lot! How much time do you think a pro basketball player spends shooting free throws, or a pro baseball player spends in the batting cage? The truth is, with golf, as with anything else, if you want to get better, then yes, you're going to have to practice.

But I'm talking about a different kind of practice here. "Practice" to many amateur golfers is just warming up. They'll go out before a round or some afternoon after work and hit a bucket of balls and call it practice. That's not the kind of practice I'm talking about. I'm talking about something much more intentional, more directed, more specific. Let me give you an example.

I was playing a round the other day with some guys at the club. The first hole is a relatively short par 4, slight dogleg to the left. It's the very first hole and the green looks close. Lots of players, including one of the guys I was playing with that day, step up and try to hit the ball as far as they can. So what happens? You guessed it. He tensed up. He wasn't fully warmed up, and he blocked the shot to the right and into the trees. Now obviously, the tee shot needs work. And yes, that's going to take some practice. But let's talk for a minute about the next shot he's got to hit from the trees on the right.

Go Get that Shot

Am I suggesting that you go out and put all your shots in the trees so you'll be able to practice that shot? Well, not exactly. But when you have some time, you should absolutely hit a few from that spot in the trees. You should go to that spot in the trees from where it always seems you are hitting. Drop a few balls and practice that shot. Don't practice the crazy, "get out of jail" shot. Practice hitting it to where you'd want to play it safe, wherever that might be.

You might say, "Well, gosh, a sixty-yard shot to get out of the trees and back to the center of the fairway is simple. I can do that!" Well, if you've never done it, how do you know you can do it? It might look easy, but you've still got to execute, you have to hit the shot. If you've never hit the shot before, there's always a big margin for error, which can create questions in your mind as you're standing over the ball.

Maybe your swing is tentative, and you don't hit it hard enough, leaving it short. Or you hit it fat and don't even get it out of the woods, or you hit it thin and punch it all the way through the fairway into the rough on the other side. The more you practice that shot, the more confidence you'll have. You'll stand over that lie in the woods knowing you can hit the shot.

There aren't a lot of teaching pros who will tell their students, "Okay, I want you to go over there into the trees because I know you're going to be in there a bunch. I want you to hit this whole bucket of balls and practice the low shot to the fairway, ninety yards from the green."

There are almost no coaches who will say that…but there should be.

Teaching pros might say, "Instead of teaching my students to hit it out of the trees, I'm going to spend the time teaching them how not to hit it there." And they're right, they should. But golfers will always end up in jail at one point or another. That's just part of the game. And the best golfers will always practice for that eventuality.

Once you become proficient at hitting the safe shot, you'll have time to practice a few of those crazy, Bubba Watson, "get out of jail" shots. You can practice hitting that forty-yard hook to within twelve feet of the hole with your wedge instead of the easy shot to the fairway.

Practice the Tough Shots

It's easy to practice the shots you like to hit. But chances are, those aren't the shots you need to practice. Like in basketball, if you're right handed, you can probably dribble pretty well with your right hand. But you'll never be a complete player until you develop the skill of dribbling and shooting with your left hand as well. Not being able to go to your left will end up handicapping your game at some point. The same is true in golf.

Let's say you're standing over a difficult shot in the club tournament. Have you ever hit a shot like the one you're attempting? No. You've never hit it, but you're going to try it. Why would you ever do that? If you don't pull off the shot, you're going to hit it in the water or over the green into the sand. Worst case scenario, you'll make a double or even a triple bogey. But, if you simply chip it out into the fairway, now you've got a ninety-yard shot that gives you a chance to get up and down and still save par, or worst case, make bogey.

Practicing shots, standing over the difficult ones and thinking through this process, is the place you need to get to in your mind. It doesn't mean you back off and never play boldly. In fact, I even talk quite a bit about playing aggressively. Practice will not only help your physical game, and it'll help you play smarter golf.

A while back I was in the gallery when my son was playing in a high school tournament. Twice, I watched as he hit his approach shot only halfway to the green. This was a shot you wouldn't usually practice, and he obviously hadn't: A fifty-yard, knock-down 7-iron from under the trees to hit a spot in the fairway. Each time, he tensed up and decelerated his swing, chunking it well short of his target. After the round, I told him, "You've got to go get that shot. You need to go out on the course and practice that shot until you've got it down. Trust me; you're going to need that shot again."

The Michelob Houston Open. Final Round, winner by 3. 1981.

Letting Out the Steam

Golf's Pressure Relief Valve

We've talked about the pressure and stress that come when folks play golf. You feel the pressure to play well. That pressure builds up causing tension, and tension is the enemy of good golf. You're tense because you're playing with people you want to impress or you simply just don't want to embarrass yourself. Or you might even be feeling pressure from the outside, pressures you can't do anything about, like trying to play in the wind or poor course conditions or even playing alongside the gum-smacking guy in your foursome who's destroying your concentration.

All that pressure manifests itself as tension, and it starts in the way you grip the club (more on that later). As we mentioned before, the tension moves from your grip through your whole body causing your swing to break down and your shot to fail.

But practice is golf's real "pressure relief valve." The more you practice the shots that cause you the most difficulty, the more confidence you'll have that you can hit the shot when you need to hit it. And that, my friend, relieves the build-up of pressure when you're standing over that ball.

When you spend time intentionally practicing those shots that give you the most trouble, you'll be much more successful quieting those voices in your head that are trying to remind you of all those bad shots you've hit over the years. You'll stand over the shot brimming with confidence because you know you can hit the shot. Practicing has a way of replacing all those negative thoughts with positive, confident ones.

The Personal Challenge

Practicing can be tough, and it can get boring. That's why I will invent challenges for myself, games to keep my mind engaged in the process. Just hitting putt after putt on the practice green can get pretty monotonous. I know teaching pros that have a two-foot flat circle they'll lay out on the practice green. Then they have their pupils putt balls from fifteen, twenty, twenty-five, and thirty feet to the two-foot "hole."

They'll challenge them by saying, "We're not leaving this green until you can get ten balls inside that circle."

Challenging yourself like this is one way to practice "pressure" and it's much better to learn how to handle the pressure in practice than to wilt under it when you're on the course. I'll also tell myself, "I'm going to make this putt for my wife." I even remember one tournament where I told myself before a putt, "I've already made a putt today for my wife. I'll make this one for my son."

Even your tough rounds of golf can become good opportunities to practice. One of my favorite sayings to anyone who asked about my round when I played poorly or didn't have the best of days was, "I sure got to practice a lot of patience out there today!"

The more you practice, the more you'll be able to "feel" what a successful shot looks like. You'll know what to think. You'll know how tightly to grip the club. You'll know how to line up your shot. You'll feel the slot when the club reaches the height of the back swing. You'll feel the contact when the club meets the ball and your follow through is just right. That's called muscle memory. In a way, you've executed that shot so much, your arms, back, hips, and legs just know what to do.

But good muscle memory only happens with repetition and routine. And routine is what happens when you practice a lot. You develop a routine, which just happens to be the very next key to Focus Golf.

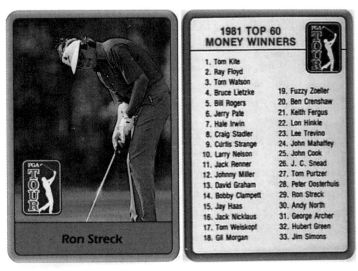

Ron Streck golf card. Money Winners, #29, Ron Streck. 1981.

6

Automatically Better

KEY #3: Developing a Routine

During the best rounds I have had on the Tour, I couldn't tell you exactly how I stood in relation to par without looking at the scoreboard or having someone tell me. I was so focused, thinking forward to each shot as it presented itself, I was able to blank out the tournament around me. This is what's called being "in the zone." No one really knows the secret of getting in the zone, but I've got an idea.

I know from experience that when I'm able to take the things I've learned from repetitive practice on the practice areas to the golf course, it builds my confidence. And nothing gets you in the zone quicker than playing with confidence. Playing good golf is all about building confidence in your game. And you build trust by developing routines through repeating the same swing, same putting stroke, the same positive concentration over and over again.

Routine Relaxes

How important is routine? Watch basketball players who are very successful at making their free throws. When I was younger, I would always dribble the ball three times then shoot. Every single time. The routine helped me to focus on the shot and drown out all the distractions from the game situation to the screams and taunts of the opposing crowd.

The same is true in golf. Good golf comes from developing the routine of doing the same thing with every shot. Any given weekend you can watch the Tour pros on television. You'll see them always go through routines on the green. They'll do the same thing over every putt. In that kind of pressure moment, a routine is the only thing that will relax you. When you can develop a routine, it will take away the tension and pressure. Again, tension is the enemy of successful golf.

One way I can always tell a person has allowed tension to take over is by noticing their grip. If I can see the whites of their knuckles as they address their shot, I know they're gripping the club way too tightly and they are not relaxed.

There was a time I was playing a round with a famous pro tennis player. We were playing at Westchester Country Club up in New York. I noticed he was squeezing the club way too tightly. He was probably a 2 or 3 handicap but the way he was playing that day, he wasn't going to break 90. He was just way too tense.

I finally asked him, "How hard do you hold the tennis racket?" He grabbed my hand like a handshake. It was just a little firmer than I hold the golf club. So while I had his hand, I demonstrated my grip for him. I said, "Here's how hard I'm holding my golf club." He was shocked. It was evident he was strangling his club.

That's what the routine will do for you. It rids you of the tension that causes you to grip the club too tightly. And as we've pointed out, the tension in your hands travels up to your neck, shoulders and back, wreaking havoc with your swing.

Make it Automatic

We talked in the last chapter about how practice develops muscle memory. But remember, it's not just practice. It's repetitive practice. It's repetition and routine that builds muscle memory. In other words, the more you build repetition and routine into your game, into your swing, the more automatic it will become. And that's the goal…to make it automatic.

When I was in college, playing on the golf team, I would hit wedges for hours just for that reason. I wanted the execution of hitting a wedge to become automatic for me. I wanted to create a feel for the club, a confidence that I knew exactly what I could do with that shot. And think about it. When do you most use your wedges? When you're around the green. And it's when you're around the green that your margin for error shrinks tremendously. That's when you need the extra help to calm your nerves that routine can bring.

Think about the road you take to go to your house. Chances are there are places along that drive where you hardly have to think at all. The path is so familiar that driving it has become practically automatic.

The same applies to hitting a golf shot. You know before you address the ball what club you have in your hand, and you know what the wind is doing, you know what kind of shot you want to hit. Now, rely on your pre-shot routine to help you clear your mind and go out and hit the shot.

If you think about it, a routine is all about consistency. If your routine isn't the same from the first hole to the 18th hole, you're not doing it right. If you take more time standing over what you believe to be a more important shot than you do a less important shot you're not developing a routine and the shot is not going to become automatic.

The Two Routines

When I talk about developing a routine, I'm actually talking about two different kinds of routines. There's the physical routine and the mental routine. The physical routine is just what you would imagine it is, and it will vary depending on the golfer. This is the physical way you approach every shot. It's how you hold the club and address the ball. It's the way you get ready to hit the shot; Whether or not you take practice swings, how high you tee the ball, how you settle yourself just before pulling back the club to begin your swing. When you can develop a routine that will work for every club and every shot, it will go a long way toward quieting the voices in your head and allowing you to relax and hit the shot you know you can make.

So, the physical routine is evident; you can easily identify it from watching others play the game. But there's more…there's the mental routine. And this is the part you can't see. This is what's going on inside the mind of the player. Just like the physical routine, the mental routine will vary depending on the golfer. Some will close their eyes to visualize the shot. Others will find a phrase or word that helps them narrow their mental focus. They will repeat that word or phrase as they address their ball and prepare to make their shot. Maybe it's "Be Aggressive" or "Nice and Easy."

As I used to stand over putts, one phrase that really helped me was "Low and Slow and in the Hole." That phrase helped me so much I had it engraved on a ball marker I used for years. We'll talk more about these expressions in the last chapter. The actual phrase doesn't matter as much as the fact that you have one. It could be "Roses are Red" for that matter. But the mental routine of saying it to yourself will help you relax.

Just Relax

We've talked about relaxation being tantamount to a successful round. And certainly, developing a routine is one sure-fire way to build the confidence that allows you to relax. But it's not the only way.

Some guys are so intense; they rarely talk to or even acknowledge those they're playing with. These guys have found that for them to locate the zone, they have to shut themselves off to everything and everyone around them. But golfers are a funny bunch. There are other golfers who seem to feed off the energy of the gallery. They're laughing and joking around, engaging not only with the guys they're playing with but also random fans along the ropes. Relaxation can look very different with different players.

Remember it's not important HOW you find the zone. It's just important that you find it. You might draw inward, or you might engage outward. But repetition and finding your physical and mental routine will go a long way toward helping you find the zone that works for you.

Front.

Back.

Medals received after tournament wins. L to R top row: San Antonio Texas Open. Michelob Houston Open. L to R bottom row: Chrysler Team Invitational. Nike Yuma Open.

7

What You See Is What You Get

KEY #4: See the Shot

Have you ever watched the best players in the world play a round of golf? Have you noticed what they do before they ever address the ball? Almost all of them will stand behind the ball and visualize the shot they want to hit.

Their senses are picking up on all the information they are going to need to hit the shot. They notice the wind in the trees, the lie of the ball, the grain of the grass. And while they are standing behind the ball, they trace the flight path they want the ball to make. They even "see" where they want the ball to land.

I've seen a lot of amateurs do this too, but there's a difference in their visualizing. In many cases, the amateurs are imagining the shot they want to hit. In other words, they imagine the shot because they've never actually hit that shot before. They haven't put in the practice time to have a memory of the great shot they're hoping to pull off now.

But the pros are different. They remember a shot they've hit well in the past that they want to duplicate now. Imagining and remembering are two very different things. When you have to imagine the shot, it's because a memory of that shot doesn't exist. You've never hit it before. You have no memory to fall back on. Of course, the problem here is that your brain will switch to a default memory, which is the one where you hit the ball into the trees on the right or hit it fat and left it short of your intended target.

Making a Deposit in Your Memory Bank

That's why practice is so important. You're not only building muscle memory; you're accruing an impressive account of great shots in your memory bank. And just like a real bank account, you can't withdraw what you don't have.

So a critical part of the mental game has its roots over on the physical side. You practice so you can create the mental images you can use later when you need to draw on that account. This memory bank, full of great shots, will not only give you a positive mental attitude as you approach your shot, but you'll also actually have a memory of the shot you've made that you can call on when you need it.

See the Putt

It's important to see your shot from the tee or the fairway, but don't forget the shots on the green, the all-important putts. In many ways, visualizing a successful putt is probably the most important thing you can do on the course.

In all my years of playing the game, one principle stands out. The only thing that really helps you putt successfully is to be able to see the ball going in the hole. You can have your favorite putter in your hands; you can have just the right grip, and just the right read of the green. But in the end, if you can't see the ball going in the bottom of the hole, you're not going to make a lot of putts. I don't care how long the putt it is or how many breaks it takes from the time it leaves the putter face. You need to see the putt going in the hole. Because once you start missing putts or lipping them out, the image of those shots not going in is going to replace all those great putts you've been imagining.

So, indeed, you practice to get better. But never forget the other reason to practice. You want to fill your memory bank with great shots you can call on right when you need them. A positive image will build confidence, which will relieve the pressure and help you relax. And when you're relaxed you'll be able to much more quickly focus on the shot you want to hit.

First TaylorMade golf bag on PGA Tour. 1979.

8

What to Say When You Talk to Yourself

FOCUS THOUGHTS: The Secret of Focus Golf

If you're standing over your shot and saying to yourself, "This one is for my son," or "Be Aggressive," or "Nice and Smooth," you've been able to take all those swirling distracting thoughts and focus them successfully into just one idea. You know the distracting thoughts I'm talking about, thoughts about the tons of tips you've seen on the Golf Channel, or worries about your grip, or club position in your swing. All of those thoughts fade into the distance when you've got a Focus Thought to take their place. It's almost like distracting your mind from all those other things and creating mental memory just like muscle memory.

One of the best tools I've used on the golf course isn't a great club or particular clothes I wear. The tool I'm talking about helps me to focus on the single shot in front of me at the time. In my pocket during a round of golf, I have many of the same things the other guys have, a ball marker, a divot tool, maybe a tee or two. But I have something else as well. My secret weapon is a tool that the others probably don't have.

My secret weapon is a simple, small piece of paper I keep in my pocket during the round. On that piece of paper, I'll have just one or two things written that will help me focus and quiet my mind while I play. I've always tried to keep these reminders focused on the mental side of the game like, "STAY POSITIVE NO MATTER WHAT" or "BE AGGRESSIVE." But sometimes I'll have a physical reminder like, "KEEP YOUR HEAD STILL." Now remember, this isn't a big sheet of paper with a long list of reminders. It's just a small piece of paper…just enough room for a thought or two.

In 2005, I won the Champions Tour Commerce Bank Championship event in New York. The first two rounds I had played well, shooting 62, 68, and I led the tournament by three shots. Before the third round, which is the final round on the Champions Tour, I entered the players' locker room to change my shoes.

When I opened my locker, I found a small note from my close friend, Mike Reid. This note simply said, "You can do this! You've done it before!" What a great encouragement. I took the note from the locker and wrote a couple of my own thoughts below his and slipped it in my pocket.

During the round, during delays or when I was waiting on my playing partner to hit, I'd pull that note out and read it over to myself. Every single time I read those words, I would relax. I'm convinced it was that note that helped me relax throughout that final round, and I was able to shoot a 67, winning the tournament by three shots.

Mental Toughness

Now you might think that was because everything had come together at one time and I magically had the physical capability that week to win. But to me, that win was a "mental toughness" win all the way. You see, I shouldn't even be playing!

I've had two knee surgeries in my life and as a result I have no ACL in my left knee. My doctors told me I would never walk normally, and they assured me that my left knee would never hold up for a career in golf. Talk about a terrible, negative thought to overcome! That's why I had to learn to lean on the side of my game where I knew I could have an advantage, the mental side. Focus Golf has allowed me to stay in the game by staying focused, relaxed, and confident.

I believe that the attitude you take to the golf course plays the biggest role in how you're going to play that day, not your clubs, not the weather, and not your competition. And I know a lot of Tour players who would agree with me wholeheartedly. Certainly, there are days when you just can't do anything wrong. We've all had those magical days when the golf gods are smiling on you and every shot you hit is the one you envisioned. But let's be honest, there are many more days when it's not like that. When everything is not going your way, and you're not hitting the shots you want to hit. These are the days you have to be mentally tough, tough enough never to give up, never.

The Focus Thoughts

In an attempt to simplify the pre-shot routine with Focus Golf, I want to give you some ideas of the kind of thoughts I'm talking about. These ideas aren't just mine. They are suggestions from other Tour pros as well. These are the thoughts they try to focus on just before they hit a drive, full shot, chip shot, sand shot, and putt.

- "Calm and Smooth"
- "Keep Your Head Still"

- "Be Aggressive"
- "Low and Slow and in the Hole"
- "See the Shot"
- "Take Away the Hands Together"
- "Positive, Aggressive Move"
- "Full Turn on Plane"
- "Stroke the Putt to the Hole"
- "Deep Breath – Exhale"
- "Have Tunnel Vision"
- "Full Swing at the Target"
- "Make This Putt for _____"
- "Never Give Up, Ever"
- "Enjoy This Ride – Now"
- "Believe in Yourself, Always"
- "I Can Do This; I've Done it Before"
- "Coil on Your Right Side"
- "Grip Pressure"
- "Make a Full Turn"
- "Mad – Positive – Aggressive"
- "Tempo"

- "Finish the Swing on Balance"
- "Watch the Ball Leave the Putter Head"
- "Focus on Target"
- "Good Rhythm"
- "Play With-IN Yourself"
- "Feel the Shot"
- "Laugh at a Bad Shot or a Bad Break"
- "Be Smooth and Always Aggressive"
- "Stay Positive No Matter What"

You may want to fill in your own ideas:

- _____
- _____
- _____
- _____
- _____

Constellation Energy Senior Players Championship, Baltimore Country Club East Course. Ron Streck hits onto the fourth green during the third round. Timonium, Maryland. 2008. (Photo by Stan Badz/PGA TOUR)

9

19th Hole

Final Thoughts

I hope these keys will "save you a sleeve of balls!"

Remember to have PASSION: The love of the game and willingness to do whatever it takes to improve.

THINK FORWARD! Take that "amnesia pill" and learn the skill of forgetting about the bad rounds and bad shots.

PRACTICE! When you practice, good things will happen. You'll develop muscle memory. You'll develop a routine, and the routine will give you confidence and help your swing or putting stroke to become automatic.

Practice will also help you RELAX. When you're able to defuse the tension, you'll play better golf. Tension can start in your grip, travel up your arms to your shoulders, neck, and back. And when your swing is infected with tension, you're never going to hit your best shot.

When you practice, you're also making deposits into your memory bank. This will allow you to SEE THE SHOT. Remember the difference between imagining the shot and remembering the shot. The more you practice, the better shots you'll be depositing into your memory bank, ready to withdraw when you need them.

Start the practice of focusing on one thought or idea. Use my secret Focus Golf weapon…a small piece of paper containing just a couple of the FOCUS THOUGHTS that resonate with you on that particular day. Stay positive and never give up. Ever!

You can play this great game your whole life, and along the way it will teach you things you cannot learn anywhere else. Honor, integrity, competition, and something you can do with anyone, any age, any gender.

So, go out there with a smile on your face and defeat someone with your hands and mind on the fairways and greens! Have FUN!

PGA TOUR

5101 RIVER ROAD   WASHINGTON, D.C. 20016   TELEPHONE: (301) 986-1550

February 4, 1977

TO: Members of the Fall 1976 Qualifying School Class

FROM: Joe Schwendeman

We thought you would like this remembrance of a very happy day.

Joe

FALL 1977 QUALIFYING SCHOOL GRADUATES

<u>Seated</u> (from left): Jim Booros, Graham Marsh, Keith Fergus, Bruce
         Ford, Mark Lye, George Kunes, Ray Sovik.

<u>Standing</u> (from left): Jay Haas, Mike Sullivan, Ron Streck, Jeff
         Mitchell, Mike Reid, Vicente Fernandez, Jim Barker,
         Alberto Rivadeneira, Larry Webb, Greg Pitzer, Rich Friedman,
         Jack Newton, Peter Jacobsen, Dick Mast, Doug Schryer.

<u>Not in picture</u>: Jim Wittenberg, John Abendroth, Bobby Stroble,
         Mark Pfeil, Dave Canipe, Don Pooley, Ray Arinno.

ABOUT THE AUTHOR

Ron Streck has been rightly named golf's Milestone Man.

Not only was Ron Streck the first PGA player to compete in sanctioned rounds with the then-revolutionary style of drivers that would become known as the "Metal Woods," but he was also the first professional player to garner a PGA Tour win with the Metal Woods.

Not only is Ron Streck the first professional golfer to win in three of the major Tours (PGA Tour, Web.com Tour, Champions Tour) but if we're counting (and of course we are counting, because as golfers, that is what we do) we would be remiss if we failed to include Ron's win on the European Tour, making Ron Streck the first professional golfer to have won on four major Tours.

Though Ron's golf accomplishments are great, he will tell you that the greatest thing of all is how God has blessed him with a wonderful wife and three wonderful children, and now grandchildren.

Because of Ron's purpose-driven life, he now plays a purpose-driven golf—Focus Golf.

If you would like to contact Ron Streck, find out more about his golf products and tips for Focus Golf, purchase books, or request him for interviews, visit:

Ron Streck

www.ronstreck.com

Ron can also be found on facebook and twitter.

Ron Streck. PGA Tour media photo.

A NOTE FROM RON STRECK

As I start this new chapter in my life with *Focus Golf with the Milestone Man,* I hope to add some laughter (it's good like medicine) and pain (it's weakness leaving the body) to the real—good and bad aspects—of life on the PGA Tour, along with stories that some would consider "inside the ropes." Or you might consider them out of bounds.

Either way, I hope you enjoy them.

My name may or may not mean anything to you, mainly depending on your age and how closely you follow the game. By way of introduction, here's a quick recap.

I'm a native of the beautiful city of Tulsa, Oklahoma, where I still reside with my wife and youngest son. I played for the University of Tulsa—college roommate of Hank Haney—and turned professional in 1976. In the forty years since, my career has taken me all over the world from Kagoshima, Japan, to Robot, Morocco, Sidney, Australia, the Fiji Islands, and all over the United States. My most notable achievement was winning at least one tournament on every Tour in which

I competed. I was fortunate enough to prevail at least once on the PGA Tour, Web.com Tour and Champions Tour while also winning late-season invitational events on the Japanese Tour and European Tour for good measure.

Being the first player to win on the three major U.S. Tours as well as the first player to hit Metal Woods in competition and win with Metal Woods (1981 Michelob Houston Open), some have dubbed me the Milestone Man.

For a long time, I had another record, the lowest 36 holes to close out an event on the PGA Tour when I shot 63, 62 in the 1978 San Antonio Texas Open to win that event by a single shot.

In 1978, during my second year on the PGA Tour, I attended a players' only meeting during the Michelob Houston Open. Commissioner Deane Beman asked if we would support a split Tour or would we rather put money towards a Senior Tour. More than 90 percent of the players voted for the Senior Tour. I was twenty-four at the time, thinking "I'm voting for something twenty-six years away." Well, those twenty-six years have flown by, yet that meeting doesn't seem so long ago. I remember the discussion and vision for the Senior Tour being about taking care of our long-time members of the Tour and creating a place for competition and income in the eve of careers. In the beginning, it was hard to get enough players to fill the fields. Not the case anymore.

When Sam Snead, Arnold Palmer, Jack Nicklaus, Lee Trevino, and others came out and supported the Tour, it became popular. It was a new place to compete for competitive warriors on a more level playing field. Hale Irwin has been by far the best on the Senior Tour, winning forty-five tournaments. Hale was pleasant enough but a real assassin on the course.

There's a lot more camaraderie and small talk on the Senior Tour (now called PGA Tour Champions). Guys will smile, say hello, and ask how you're doing and where you're staying. Yet there are still guys who privately wish you would shoot 80 each round and couldn't care less if you're staying on the back porch at the Ratview Inn.

Golf is a humbling sport for even the greatest to have ever played. It develops character in a person that carries through life. Players are taught the rules at a very young age. You call penalties on yourself even when no one is watching. You count all your shots even if the ball moves on you while your club is grounded. We don't see baseball players turning around to the umpire and saying, "I think that was a strike; you called it a ball." Or a football player telling the referee he was holding on that play. In basketball, a player runs over a guy and the official has to determine whether it's a charging foul or blocking foul, then the announcers argue about it. In golf, you can try to fudge on the rules, but it won't get you very far.

Another difference in golf—from most other sports—no guarantees. You are paid by how you perform, not by how someone thinks you will perform.

The amount today players are paid has certainly changed. I spoke with Arnold a couple years ago and he told me that in 1960 he won the Canadian Open and first place was $2,000. Now, you have to earn nearly one million dollars just to keep your Tour card as one of the Top 125. Hard to fathom, but hey, who's counting?

Golf is fun. Period. I'm elated to have this opportunity to be candid and share some of my stories and golf tips through my *One-Putt* column and through Focus Golf. I'd love to hear from you, so please feel free to reach out to me and I will do my best to answer any general or specific questions on the game or even past tournaments.

I've had the fortune of finding my way into playing (and winning) professional golf in four separate decades: I started playing when Nicklaus was in his prime; Tom Watson was just becoming one of the great players; And some of the "greats" were getting older—guys like Snead were playing every once in a while. I played with Sam at Quad Cities the first two rounds. He was sixty-six years old and shot a 66 in the first round. I'll always remember seeing the gleam in his eyes that day.

Yours truly,
Ron Streck
Milestone Man
www.ronstreck.com
contact@ronstreck.com

** With the fondest memories and gratitude for
golf's greatest ambassador, "The King." **
ARNOLD PALMER
10 SEPT 1929 ~ 25 SEPT 2016
YOU set the standard.